Get MORE Out of LIFE

Julie Lother   Joan Kennedy

Written by a **39**-year-old and a **92**-year-old

ISBN 978-1503325197

Library of Congress Cataloging-in-Publication Data

Printed in the United States of America

Contact

Joan Kennedy

+1 651-528-8761

jvkennedy1@aol.com

www.joankennedy.com

Julie Lother

+1 651-235-5546

Julie@fit-2b-well.com

www.fit-2b-well.com

Designed by Voom Creative, Inc.

I would like to dedicate this book to my
dad Rob, grandma Norriene, husband Brent
and children, Dianna and Aaron.

- Julie

To my children, Bob, Marnie, Patty and Amy, who bring
so much love, joy and humor to my life.

- Joan

Preface

On Meeting Each Other – Julie's Story

I was on the Professional Women's Network board and invited Joan to come in as the keynote speaker. The group of women was mostly entrepreneurs looking to grow their businesses. Her talk was about her experience in losing her house and everything she owned, but not giving up on life. She was selling her book "What's Age Got to Do With it?" and I bought one because of her tenacity at age 86 and her still being in the business world. I was impressed! I wan't sure if I would read the book since I was only in my early 30s and ready to have a baby in two months. Plus, it was about aging. Heck, I was young, pregnant and worrying about how I was going to be a parent. Why would I read a book on aging? Well, to my surprise, this book and Joan changed my life. I set the book aside, had my baby, and learned that my job was eliminated in a matter of six months. I picked up Joan's book because her talk was positive and uplifting. As I read the book, I was highlighting most of the pages because it was all good. The quote that I still remember and say to this day is, "Thinking the right thoughts is the basis of all accomplishments, success, self-confidence, and happiness."

After I read the book and applied parts of it to my life, I was inspired. I thought, "Wow, this 86-year-old needs to know how her book has helped me!" I e-mailed Joan to tell her how grateful I was to have read her book and asked if she wanted to meet for coffee so I could personally express my gratitude in words. She said yes! We met at a Starbucks, and when I walked in she was all dressed in white, looking very sharp and glowing with energy. I gave her a big hug and the rest is history. Since then, we've been meeting, sharing stories about life, and writing this book.

....

Embrace fully your capacity to create,
to think in unlimited ways, and pursue
everything you have been wanting.

....

~ Sanaya Roman Duane Packer

I want
MORE

1

We all want more! In fact, would we have any difficulty at all making an extensive list: more love, more success, more fun, more closet space? Now what if you were asked another question: "What do you think is your biggest obstacle to get more out of life?" Would your answer be "myself," or, more importantly, "my innerself?"

There is someone you spend more time with than anyone else, someone who has more influence over you, more potential to help or harm you, and the ability to obstruct or support your growth, than anyone else. This ever-present companion is your innerself.

You experience the innerself as a distinct person talking to you. You engage this person in an ever-constant dialogue, such as, "I don't have the confidence in myself to do that." "Nothing is working out for me." "Nothing is going to change for me." "I'll never be able to do that." What we say to ourselves becomes our reality.

It is through this internal dialogue that you make decisions, set goals, feel pleased and satisfied, depressed or unfulfilled. Your feelings and your self-image are influenced by your innerdialogue. Conversely, your self-image (to be discussed in chapter two) influences your self-talk. However, changing your inner dialogue can be the first step in improving your self-image.

We all talk to ourselves constantly, whether we know it or not. Self-talk plays a key role in determining how you act and how you feel about yourself. Your thoughts and words determine the direction and quality of your life. Our self-talk can make the difference between happiness and despair, between self-confidence and self-doubt. So the question is, "What have you been telling yourself today?" Have you worried about your future, nagged yourself about your past, criticized yourself for making a mistake, for making the wrong decision, or have you complimented and supported yourself?

If you don't remember what you've said to yourself today, you're not alone. Self-talk is so familiar to you that you are barely aware of it. You can think thousands of thoughts each day and it's the negative self-talk that limits your ability to make positive changes in your life. What you think is critical – your thoughts will either energize you or immobilize you.

You have within you the power to overcome self-doubt – this powerful tool will enable you to improve your self-image and attain positive self-talk. This wonderful power dwells within you. It is the subconscious mind that creates your life according to how it has been programmed. It equips you with the necessary elements, qualities, and potential to make your life the one you truly want to live.

Your subconscious mind is at work 24 hours every day, 365 days a year. It accepts the instructions from your conscious mind.

Joan's story

Years ago, I enjoyed reading Family Circle Magazine. My favorite part was the column called Butternut Wisdom, written by Gladys Taber. In her column each month, she wrote about her cottage in Stillmeadow. Her kitchen was filled with gleaming copper pots and pans, grey stoneware, and the aroma of bread baking in the oven. "But the best part," she said, "was the creek that flowed past my cottage." In the spring she planted flowers along its banks. Each month, Gladys Tabor painted a picture of absolute pure joy for me.

I started telling my family, and boring my friends, with the often-repeated phrase, "One day I'm going to live in a house by a creek."

Years passed, and I moved to the east coast. When I returned home, the first thing I did was visit my dad, who lived in a small town in Wisconsin. While I was there, my dad asked me to come and live with him. The last thing I wanted to do at the time was to live in a small town. That was not a part of my plans. After thinking a great deal about it, I finally said yes, and moved to Neillsville, Wisconsin.

In the spring of the first year, I was sitting in my bedroom looking out of the window at O'Neil Creek. Suddenly it dawned on me – I was living in a house by a creek. The only problem was, when I said I wanted to live in a house by a creek, I should have been more specific. There I was, years later, living in a house by a creek, but there was a service road between the house and the creek. No chance at all of planting flowers along its banks.

There has to be the awareness that things happen in your mind before they can happen in your life. The conditions under which you live are a result of your thought processes. An honest inventory of what you have in your everyday life will give you a good idea of the kind of thinking in which you have engaged. The subconscious mind can bring you the things you desire in life, like success, confidence, love, and peace of mind. It can also bring you failure, frustration, fear, and self-doubt.

It's important to manage your self-talk. One of the goals of this book is to help you realize how much of your internal dialogue is negative, and how to replace those negative thoughts with positive thoughts.

Thoughts to Energize You:

- There is someone you spend more time with than anyone else. This ever-present companion is your innerself.

- You think thousands of thoughts each day. Reflect on the positive thoughts and make positive changes in your circumstances or in your life.

- You are equipped with the necessary elements, qualities, and potential to make your life the one you truly want to live.

- Success, happiness and a great future are all around you and can be yours, depending on what you think and say each day to yourself and to others.

....

You are unlike anyone
who has ever lived, but
that uniqueness isn't
a virtue, it's a
responsibility.

....

~ Mark Batterson

Make the **MOST** of **YOURSELF**

2

Regardless of your position or circumstances, you can take control of your life. Anyone who would like to improve the conditions of his or her life can do so with only one prerequisite – the desire to change.

You may be happy with family, friends, even your employer. You may only have the desire to change things about yourself – things that weigh you down and impede your progress toward career goals. But before any real changes can take place in your life, you need to search within. Become aware of who you are and what is possible. You will never know who you really are until you deal with the person you think you are.

You may not be consciously aware of it, but you carry within you a mental image of the kind of person you think you are. You've built this image from all your experiences, your successes and failures, and from the way people have reacted toward you, especially in your childhood. Once an idea about yourself goes into this image, it becomes true, as far as you are concerned. You will act like the kind of person you think you are. You cannot act any other way.

High self-image is something every person needs. You need it because it is the very core of your being and because it increases your chances of finding happiness in life. Your self-image affects how you see the world and your place in it. It also directs you in the choices you make about what you will do with your life.

At this very moment, your self-image is either your greatest asset or your greatest liability. Nothing is as important to your psychological well-being as the level of your self-image.

In self-talk, rarely do people say positive things about themselves. For some of us, the thoughts we are thinking today are the same thoughts we had yesterday and the day before. Ask yourself, "To what am I giving power?" It could be negative thoughts like, "Nothing seems to be working out for me." "Every time I get a little money ahead, something happens." "Everything happens to me." "I just don't seem to get anywhere." "I'm at a loss as to what to do." By the hundreds, these messages flash across our minds. A result of this negative feedback is low self-image. Your thoughts determine who you are, what you are, and what you will become.

It is essential that you consciously discard the negative phrases and thoughts, as they bring you the very opposite of what you want.

You need to be aware, at all times, that you have an incredible power within you. This power is your subconscious mind. Whatever you feed your subconscious mind, true or false, negative or positive, will register as the truth. Every time you maintain a negative destructive thought, you are actually asking your mind to create that kind of condition in your life.

You need to be aware, at all times, that the subconscious mind is listening. It is impersonal and treats everything you say with the same indifference. It accepts and obeys, and it brings back to you the things you think about, talk about, and believe to be true. If you want this powerful, creative mind to work in your favor, you need to stop giving it the wrong commands.

Thought is the most dynamic, most creative element you have to work with, but if it isn't controlled, it can be the most destructive force in your life. Here is the good part. The subconscious mind is so powerful and so subject to suggestion, that in affirmations, you have a tool of extraordinary power. You can raise your self-image and thereby raise your potential. You can literally change the course of your life by changing your thinking.

Julie's story

Internal inspiration equals external results. This is the motto I live by. If you believe in yourself and practice positive thinking and affirmations, you will receive external gratification. If you are trying to lose weight but you keep telling yourself, "I can't lose weight," that's what will happen. Internal inspiration is where a healthy you begins. Want positive and healthy results? Believe in yourself.

One of the clients whom I was training for two months would repeatedly say, "Julie, I am not losing any weight. Why isn't this working?" I kept reminding her to focus on her daily accomplishments rather than get overwhelmed by her overall goal, focus on what is working, and affirm her intention. Indeed, she did just that! She lost over 20 pounds, and most importantly, she feels good about herself.

Positive thinking is all about using positive affirmations – short, positive statements that you repeat to yourself regularly. Or you can write some affirmations down on cards and leave them around the house where you will regularly see them.

Positive affirmations must:

- Always be positive.

- Be in the present tense.

- State your intentions or wants.

- Be brief so you can remember and repeat.

Many times you try to remake the external world around you, forgetting that the place you have most influence is in your own life.

Through affirmations, you can make changes in yourself and in your circumstances. You need to phrase your affirmations in the present tense, such as, "I am well organized," rather than, "I'm going to get organized." This moment "now," is our point of power.

The first of the affirmations is, "I love myself unconditionally." Begin the habit of saying affirmations every day. In time, you may begin to notice a little more vitality and energy. Soon you will see indications that circumstances are beginning to change. You will see new ways to manage a challenge or solve a problem.

When you are ready to make your affirmations, sit in a relaxed position. Sitting is suggested so that you are less likely to fall asleep. Listen to your body and focus on the muscles that seem tense. Take a few deep breaths, and when you feel relaxed, begin your affirmations.

You can start by choosing five affirmations and say those for about a month, then add others to your list. The affirmations below are the foundation for change. You need to like yourself, and it's also important to like others and allow others to be themselves as well. It takes about three weeks to change a habit, and the same amount of time to form a new habit.

Say your affirmations every day, and then add new affirmations.

A list of positive affirmations:
- I love myself unconditionally.

- I have warm regards for all people at all times.

- I am 100 percent alive by thinking, speaking, and acting with great enthusiasm.

24

- I am completely relaxed and self-assured in all situations and with all people.

- I am well organized in every phase of my life.

It's important to make only positive statements when talking about yourself. Eliminate all the negative ones that you are in the habit of saying. Through affirmations, you can raise your self-image and raise your potential.

If you say daily affirmations even for a short time, they will bring satisfying results in your life. When you firmly believe the best is still within you, you will become empowered.

Thoughts to Energize You:

- You will never know who you really are until you deal with the person you think you are.

- At this very moment, your self-image is either your greatest asset or your greatest liability.

- Internal inspiration equals external results.

- I am energized and alive.

More positive affirmations for you to use:

- I am healthy and happy.

- Wealth is pouring into my life.

- My body is healthy and functioning in a very good way.

- I have a lot of energy.

- I study and comprehend fast.

- My mind is calm.

- I am calm and relaxed in every situation.

- My thoughts are under my control.

- I radiate love and happiness.

- I am surrounded by love.

- I have the perfect job for me.

- I am living in the house of my dreams.

- I have a loving relationship with
  my wife/husband.

- I have a wonderful and satisfying job.

- I am successful in whatever I do.

- Everything is getting better every day.

- I am getting better every day, in every way.

....

Would you tell me please,
which way I ought to go from here?"
"That depends a good deal on where
you want get to," said the cat.
"I don't much care where,"
said Alice. "Then it doesn't matter
which way you go," said the cat.

....

~ *Conversation between Alice and the Cheshire Cat*
From "Alice in Wonderland"

Raise your
EXPECTATIONS

3

In the three stages of life, childhood, young adult, and maturity, the third stage is recognized today as the period where people really grow. It is time to realize that you can no longer wait to decide if you are achieving your life goals. It is time to evaluate what you have done and what you still want to do.

The important thing is not where you were, or even where you are, but where you want to be in the future. Without a doubt, when you plan for a vacation, you always know exactly where you are going, how you will travel, and what it will cost. You would never waste time driving around aimlessly until your vacation was over, yet so many people do just that with their lives. The problem is, they haven't set a course because they haven't determined their destination.

Although goals are vital to our well-being, many of us continue to live without them. We live life as it comes along, one day at a time. It's called free fall.

> Whatever happens ... happens.
> You have to take life as it happens,
> but you should try to make it happen
> like you want to take it.
>
> *- Old German saying*

There is no purpose or vitality to your life without goals. It's important to have something in your future to look forward to, to aspire to. If you don't, you will come to a point in your life when you begin to look to the past, and view that time as the time you did all your living.

Life holds no real success until you find that which fulfills you. The most important question you can ask yourself is, "What do I want to do in my life above everything else?" Goals give purpose to the way you spend your days. They create an anticipation for life, and they give your life direction.

Once you decide on a life changing goal, you can't allow leftover fears or doubts to get in your way. You may have had negative experiences that hurt or disappointed you. These experiences may cause you to doubt your abilities. Your tendency to focus on the negative aspects of life only helps to impress the negative occurrences deeper in your mind. In remembering your failures, you are reliving them and making them your present. When you dwell on failure, it is failure that you will achieve.

Fear and faith are the greatest factors competing for control of your mind, especially when setting and achieving goals. Fear is a powerful force. It keeps you from asserting yourself. It persuades you to set easier goals. Fear keeps you from taking the risks necessary for changing your life.

Without a doubt, you've had inspired moments, when you see clearly how you could do a certain thing, but you don't have enough confidence in yourself, or in your idea, to make it a reality. Then sooner or later, someone else comes along, with no more ability or background, and does the very thing you only thought of doing.

Often when you see a very successful person, you may think she or he has a special gift that you don't have. Actually, the greatest gift is their ability to take action. To succeed in life, to do the things you want to do, to have the things you want to have, your mind must focus steadily on what you want, not on what you don't have. Whatever your mind holds onto will become reality in your life. Have you ever told yourself that someday, when the time is right, you are going to do what you've always wanted to do? Unfortunately, for some, that day never comes. You may have many reasons why you can't do it just yet. Excuses and your inner negative dialogue keep you from doing the things you really want to do.

You find yourself saying, "How can I possibly do everything I need to do today?" "The things I do aren't necessarily the things I want to do." "I'm just too busy to get things done." Many times, when you think you are giving reasons for not doing something, what you are actually doing is giving excuses. It doesn't matter what kind of excuse you use – just one can keep you from doing the things you really want to do.

Every day, thousands of people bury good ideas because they are afraid to act on them, or they procrastinate. Tomorrow, next week, later, or someday are often synonymous with never. Ask yourself: "Why do I put things off, make excuses, or let anyone or anything get in the way of my commitments?" And what do you say to yourself when you do not complete what is important to you?

When people look back over their lives, they regret actions and risks not taken far more than the mistakes they made, even the big ones.

You don't have to do everything today, but you have to do something every day. You have to keep moving forward in order to keep your dreams alive. When you have no specific plans for getting anywhere, you always have lots of reasons to explain why you don't, why you can't, and why you haven't. When you are uncertain, you do nothing.

Fear can play a big part in the decision to do something today or put it off until tomorrow. You have to face the fact that no philosophy will help you to achieve, if you doubt your ability to do so. No matter how hard you work for success, if your thoughts are filled with the fear of failure, they will paralyze you.

In every major decision you may be in conflict with yourself ... whether to act or not to act. If you are not aware of this, indecision can become habitual and it will prevent you from taking constructive steps.

You can do several things to avoid the tendency of waiting until conditions are just right before you act:

• Accept the possibility that there may be future obstacles and difficulties.

- Don't waste time beforehand worrying about those possibilities.

- When you have a problem, you always have two options: worry about it or solve it.

- Don't harbor doubts about the decision once it's made.

- Start each day with the conviction that many new ideas will come to you, which will provide unusual opportunities.

- Trust your instincts.

Remember, you cannot think success and failure at the same time. One or the other will dominate. It's imperative that you get rid of thoughts of past failures. When you finally come to a decision, you just need to stay with it.

Thoughts to Energize You:

- Goals create an anticipation for life, and they give your life direction.

- To succeed in life, to do the things you want to do, to have the things you want to have, your mind must focus steadily on what you want.

- Do something every day. Keep moving forward in order to keep your dreams alive.

- When you reach a decision, just stay with it.

....

Remember, someday doesn't exist,
never has, and never will.
There is no "Someday."
There is only today.
When tomorrow comes,
it will be another day, so will the next day.
There is never anything but today.

....

~ Jeff Olson

Just GET it DONE

4

"Everybody builds a dream in their lifetime," says Christopher LaBret. "You're either going to build your dream, or somebody else's. So build your own."

Joan's story

In the spring of the first year with my dad, he asked me if I wanted to learn to 'make garden.' I thought I could handle a small garden. So I agreed. He then gave me a number to call, which I did. The following Saturday, the farmer arrived with his rototiller. He used it to cut a 75-by-50 foot swath in the back yard, which to me looked as big as a football field.

"Somebody has got to be kidding," were the only words I could utter. "How can I possibly plant that entire garden, much less weed it?" My dad had a way of ignoring stupid questions. So there was my first lesson: "You do whatever it takes to get the job done."

While my dad stood by with his walker, watching me, I began planting three long rows of potatoes, two rows of onions, two rows of carrots, four short rows of corn, tomatoes, peppers, lettuce, cucumbers, zucchini, and garlic.

The carrots, onions, and corn never made an appearance. My dad said, "You planted them too deep." The garlic didn't show up either. He said, "You probably planted them upside down." The zucchini blew up like a balloon and daily the rabbits and I were in a heated race to see who would have lettuce for lunch. On a scale of one to ten, my first attempt at gardening drew a miserable four as far as my dad was concerned. He was disappointed and I breathed a sigh of relief after harvest.

The following spring, my dad said, "Are we going to 'make garden' this spring?" I said, "It's okay with me, if it isn't too big." However, neither one of us informed the farmer we were planning on a smaller garden this year. Much to my chagrin, I ended up with the same size garden as the previous year ... 75-by-50 feet.

I left for Peoria, Illinois to speak to the American Business Women's Association. Leaving behind a standing ovation from over 650 women, I returned home. As I drove up to the house, a huge mound of black dirt greeted me. Luggage in hand, I went into the house. I said, "Dad what's all that black dirt doing in the back yard?" "That's not black dirt," he said, "that's manure."

He then gave me his action plan. I was to purchase a spade from the Farmer's Coop and buy five pounds of onion sets and 10 pounds of seed potatoes. I hadn't even unpacked from my trip. "I don't believe this is happening to me," is a phrase I was to repeat many times over in the days to come. The second lesson: "When you have the plan, you're in control. The first thing I found out about manure is that you can't shovel it … it just clumps. My dad said, "Use the spade, that's what it's for." For the next solid week I dumped, spread and grumbled. To add to the agony, the wheel came off the wheelbarrow in the middle of the garden. More grumbling as I replaced the nut on the wheel and continued with my task.

Finally on the last day, I got up early to increase my efforts. I was not happy. Then I realized all week I had been working on my dad's goal. That was a big 'aha.' Then and there, I decided to make my dad's goal my goal. After spreading manure on the entire garden, I would give myself a reward. It worked for me. I had more energy and enthusiasm for getting the job done than I'd had the entire week.

Due to all the effort and the manure, we had a beautiful garden that flourished all summer. Best of all, my dad was happy with the outcome.

I turned 60 that summer and I knew that if I could plant a 75-by-50 foot garden by myself, I could do just about anything I set my mind to do.

Setting goals gives purpose to the way you spend your day. They create an anticipation for life, and they give your life direction. Knowing what you want eliminates indecision and confusion. Ask yourself:

- What do I want to take place in my life next week, next month, six months from now, one year from now?

- What problems do I want solved?

- What do I want to accomplish?

- What have I always wanted to do?

- What have I always wanted to learn?

When you decide on the goal you want, there are basic steps to follow to achieve your objective.

First of all, you need to have a strong desire. Desire is the motivating force in you. Without it, nothing can be achieved. You don't know the means by which the subconscious mind uses everything within reach to change your desire into reality. Desire is the starting point and the foundation of achievement. To desire deeply is to have singleness of purpose. And then follow the Five Step Plan:

- **Put your goals in writing.** Whatever you want should be written out as a clear statement of what you want to achieve. The written statement provides a solid base from which to unlock the door between daydreams and reality. In the process of writing down your goals, you have made a commitment.

- **Be specific.** It is essential that you avoid general statements, such as more money (a dollar is more money). Write the amount you desire. If your goal is a career, you need to write down exactly what you want. The mind needs a blueprint of your goals. The written words are your blueprint.

- **Determine a timeframe.** It is important to decide on the length of time it will take to achieve your goals. If you fail to consider the timeframe, it can cause you to give up too soon. A timeframe gives you a sense of urgency.

- **Don't discuss your goals with others, unless they include a special person or family member.** Talking at length about your plans and goals can diminish your motivation. Sharing your plans with others also creates pressure for you to meet their expectations and makes it difficult to change your mind. Talking about your plans may invite opinions that can inhibit you from taking action.

- **Picture your goals.** Using your imagination to create a picture in your mind and visualizing yourself in the possession of your goal is important. If your goal is a particular job, see yourself working in that position. If it's a place you want to visit, picture yourself in that location.

> Your imagination is your
> preview of life's coming attractions.
> *-Albert Einstein*

Writing your goals on an index card will prove beneficial. It's important to read your goals first thing in the morning and last thing at night.

When you have your goals clearly defined, it's important to develop the feeling of expectation.

A dynamic and enjoyable way to create great expectations is to use actual pictures. You can lay out your future in a scrapbook or loose-leaf notebook. These pictures are your Goal Book and should exemplify:

- The person you want to become.

- The home you wish to live in.

- The car you want to drive.

- The wardrobe you want to have.

- The places you want to visit.

- The career or profession you want to have.

To make your Goal Book effective, look through it each night and as many times as you can during the day. This is one way of developing a strong feeling of expectation.

After you've decided on your goal and have followed the Five Step Plan, you will need to start with a written plan, but the plan doesn't have to take you all the way to your goal. It's important to come up with a plan that will get you out of the starting gate.

> If you don't know where you are going, you'll probably end up some place else.
>
> *-Yogi Berra, Baseball Legend*

Place a written copy of your plan where you can see it daily. Make the changes as ideas come to you.

The following list of reminders will help keep you focused:

- Write out your plan. Each day do at least one task toward accomplishing it.

- Pace yourself to get the best results, and remember you are not in competition with any-one else.

- Keep your inner dialogue positive.

- Prepare for whatever you asked for, even when there is no sign of it.

- Always keep your mind on your goal, not on the obstacles.

- Each day say to yourself, "I have the talents and abilities to achieve my goal."

- Visualize your goal each night before you go to sleep, and always picture it in the present tense.

- If your goal is to be reached in a minimum amount of time, every day must count.

You need to decide on your priorities for each day. Your daily list of things to do for the following day can be written each morning or in the evening.

The list should include tasks that might be put off, if they were not written down. When making out your daily list, an important consideration is that at least one task for the day should pertain to your goal.

After the list is completed, number each task in order of importance, then start with number one and stay with it until it is completed. If, for some reason, it cannot be completed, move on to number two.

Your daily list isn't etched in stone. If there are uncompleted tasks on your list by the end of the day, they can be added to the list for the following day, in order of their importance for that day. To write or type your list in a journal, notebook, phone, or tablet is important. This will not only provide you with a record of what you have accomplished each day, but it will be easier to keep track of than a scrap of paper.

To simplify your life you need to:

- Know what it is you really want.

- Write it down.

- Analyze what you have to do to achieve it.

- Make a plan.

It's important to plan your activities for each day. Do one thing at a time so that with every small success you will become more confident. In this manner, with each passing day, you will assume control of your life. You will realize that the difference between success and failure hinges on whether you do something today or tomorrow. So, it isn't what you think about, talk about, or plan to do, it's what you actually do each day that determines your future. And finally, whatever you believe you can do, can be done.

Thoughts to Energize You:

- Desire is the motivating force within you.

- To desire deeply is to have singleness of purpose.

- All the things that now exist in your life were once simply ideas in your consciousness.

- It isn't what you think about, talk about, or plan to do; it's what you actually do each day that determines your future.

- Whatever you believe you can do, can be done.

....

Until you value yourself,
you won't value your time.
Until you value your time,
you will not do anything with it.

....

~M. Scott Peck, Author

GET on
with **IT**

5

In establishing your major goal, you have set a course for your life and have determined what you will do each day to achieve your objective. Sometimes a goal will seem too far in the future. It may seem that you never will achieve it, and you might fall back into your old time-consuming habits.

You may belong to several groups and organizations that expect you to give some of your time to committee work or meetings. You may feel that you must attend luncheons, parties, and shopping excursions at the mall. Unexpected interruptions also make demands on your time. People dropping in, telephone calls, text messages and social media, coupled with routine activities, can prevent you from having the extra time to pursue a major goal. You can get involved in activities or projects to please others, even when you don't really want to do them. It's up to you to decide whether or not you want to eliminate some of the non-productive things you find the time to do. If you can be selective in saying "yes," and comfortable with saying "no," you will have the time and energy to do what you want to do.

If you don't consciously choose how you spend your precious time on this earth, you lose it to the nonessential tasks or in spending your life meeting other people's needs.

The first step in making changes is the decision to change – to decide you want more out of life, that you want something else in your life. You need to make the decision to eliminate all the non-essential activities you may have become involved in over the years, things that take up time and do nothing for you. One of the problems you may have is putting things off.

> Do you know what happens when you give a procrastinator a good idea? Nothing.
>
> *- Donald Gardner*

You will not get bogged down by your domestic obligations while handling your job and working toward your goals, if you:

- Start each day with a positive affirmation.

- Plan each day.

- Exercise.

- Start each day a little earlier.

- Delegate tasks (anyone over six).

- Reduce social media and internet time, limit checking phone for texts and emails.

- Eliminate all unproductive work.

- Employ less rigid housekeeping habits.

Keeping track of the time spent on these activities can determine how much time you waste on time-consuming, non-productive activities, and how much time you are directing toward your highest priorities. List them as:

- Daily routine activities.

- The non-productive things you do.

Then, record the most productive tasks you do each day. If your goal is going to be reached in a minimum of time, every day must count.

Thoughts to Energize You:

- If you can be selective in saying "yes," and comfortable with saying "no," you will have the time and energy to do what you want to do.

- The first step in making changes is the decision to change – to decide you want more out of life and you want something else in your life.

- No matter how busy you feel you are, it is vital that you take the time to plan each day.

- If your goal is going to be reached in a minimum of time, every day must count.

....

I visualized where I wanted to be,
what kind of player I wanted to become.
I knew exactly where I wanted to go,
and I focused on getting there.

....

~Michael Jordan

FOCUS
or FAIL

---- **6** ----

Achievement calls for three qualities. You must be decisive, persistent, and have the ability to concentrate on your goals. It is possessing these three qualities that separates men and women who merely think about doing from men and women of action. When you have the urge to do something, you must act. Without action, nothing happens.

You may have good intentions when you say you are "going to" do something. But "going to" can imply next week, next month, or next year. Change "going to" to "I will." Saying "I will" keeps you in the present tense and creates a sense of urgency.

Do the thing and you shall have the power.

-Ralph Waldo Emerson

You may have a project ahead of you about which you are not quite certain. Your plan of action is not fully worked out, and there remains doubt as to how you are going to proceed. You hesitate until you can see your way more clearly. Unfortunately, reluctance to start anything is a weakness.

It is the inability to make a decision as to what you want or what to do that keeps you from achieving. To make any changes, to accomplish anything, you need to put aside all further reviewing and come to a decision. The more you deliberate about the best way to get started, the less likely you are to get started at all. Any decision you make will not be firm until you do something about it, and the longer you put off doing something, the more shaky your decision becomes.

Beginning a project or activity is only half of the formula for achievement. Getting things finished once you've started is largely a matter of persistence and motivation. To develop persistence and maintain motivation is a matter of:

- Making a decision without hesitation.

- Having once made the decision, not wasting time reviewing it.

- Acting promptly on the decision.

- Maintaining incentive by keeping your goal constantly before you.

- Making positive affirmations regarding the project or activity. Use the words "I enjoy" frequently, rather than "I hate" or "I dislike."

To manage your tasks, you need to concentrate. Without the power of concentration, task management is impossible. If you lack the power of concentration, you will fall prey to every whim. If you possess it, you are in control. Concentration is focusing attention on one objective and refusing to consider anything that is not pertinent to your objective.

There are many examples of a lack of concentration. Working from home is a great idea but requires discipline. You may have planned to spend your morning answering emails and making phone calls. But as you sit at your desk contemplating how best to answer a client, your mind prefers to wander and you gladly stand up and straighten the picture, water your plants, and straighten your desk. Then it's time for coffee! In the meantime, you have strayed far from your original objective of answering emails and making phone calls. An intense interest in the objective or activity is essential for concentration.

When you are absorbed in a particular project, you are oblivious to everything around you. Concentration and singleness of purpose are closely related. If you lack interest, concentration is almost impossible.

It is difficult to focus all your attention on an objective that is vague. The more definite you can make your objective, the easier it will be to concentrate. If your objective is fuzzy, if there is an elusive quality about it, then concentration is difficult. You must have something you can hold on to. Your objective must be clear-cut. This can be done by breaking it down and concentrating on a small part at a time.

Joan's story

I spent several years writing two-minute transcripts for a radio feature. One day it occurred to me that I could write a book simply by compiling these transcripts. For the next six months, I did everything but write the book. One of the problems was that I never seemed to find the time to sit down each day and write. I continued to gather data for the book – two boxes full. I made notes – in my car, restaurants, during the night, and early in the morning.

One day, I realized that the idea of writing a book was too overwhelming. I couldn't seem to concentrate. When I finally did sit down to write, I ended up filling the wastebasket faster than I filled a page. I found my thoughts wandering. Everything became a distraction. Then, one day, I had a conversation with a friend, who had written several books. I told him about my struggle to write. He said, "When you write a book, don't start with chapter one. Just start writing." Once I stopped thinking about how to start chapter one, I had no problem concentrating.

When you doubt your ability to succeed in any project on which you're trying to concentrate, you will find it difficult to focus your attention.

Like most characteristics, the extent of your power to concentrate is an acquired habit. To strengthen your ability, you have to maintain a deep interest in your objective. This will motivate you to act, regardless of feelings of inadequacy and frustration.

Success is predictable when you:

- Write down, each day, the five or more important tasks or projects you want to accomplish.

- Do something each day that pertains to your goals.

- Spend some time each day on positive affirmations.

- Eliminate thoughts of doubt in regard to achieving your goals.

- Forget past mistakes and failures.

- Persist in spite of obstacles.

Success in life is a matter not so much
of talent or opportunity, as of concentration
and perseveration.

- C.W. Wendt

That's why it's important to plan each day and concentrate only on top priorities. When you extend yourself into other activities, you weaken your power to achieve your objectives. Focus on one goal at a time instead of scattering your efforts, and you will realize your dream.

Thoughts to Energize You:

- Saying "I will" keeps you in the present tense and creates a sense of urgency.

- Take action and something will happen.

- Plan and concentrate only on top priorities.

- Stop thinking about how to start, just start.

....

Never forget that the body
is the temple of the soul.

....

~Dr. Oz

MOVE it
or LOSE it

---- **7** ----

Since your health is your number one asset, you must take care of it. Your physical energy (exercise) is the foundation of your emotional health, mental health, and spiritual health. Exercise not only makes you healthy and has unlimited benefits, it creates a positive attitude toward life.

Julie's story

I've never heard any of my clients say that they regretted exercise. Ok, maybe just one ... my husband, when I trained him that one time. Although, I can't say he is my client since he willingly allowed me to put him through a tough workout

GET MORE OUT OF LIFE

and didn't pay for the training. My longest client, whom I've been training for over nine years, says she still "hates exercise," but never regrets it. She has showed up twice a week for nine years because she knows it's good for her health (physically, mentally, and emotionally). A few years back her husband said to me, "Whatever you are doing, continue it. She is a happier person."

Everyone is different in what type of exercise they enjoy. It may be Yoga, weight training, Zumba, swimming, running, etc. Remember Newton's First Law of Motion: An object at rest stays at rest and an object in motion stays in motion. Just like when you exercise. Once you start, and you are feeling the effects of exercise, it's easy to keep going. Once you stop and lose momentum, it's easy to just quit. The body achieves what the mind believes. This is where the mind kicks in. When your mind stays in motion thinking positive thoughts, you will achieve positive results. What's good for the body is good for the brain and vice versa.

What you enjoy makes you happy. Happiness comes from within, and when you do something you enjoy, you are more likely to make it part of your day. I like the saying, "How you start your day is how you live your day." And how you live your day is how you live your life.

Starting your day with exercise will keep you in motion all day. Ten minutes or 10 push-ups are better than nothing at all. You'll feel good about the accomplishment and for taking care of yourself first.

Exercise is the key. It not only makes you healthy and has many benefits, it creates a positive attitude toward life. Because your health is your number one asset, you must take care of it.

For optimum energy, you need to seek out people who motivate you, who are cheerful, who listen to you, and who make you feel good. The worst thing you can do for your health ... is nothing.

Without your health, there is very little you can do. With health, you have options. You can be productive, set and achieve goals, stay socially active, travel, and stay in the mainstream of life.

To keep the health you now have, stay positive, eat well, exercise, and laugh a lot. Evidence indicates laughter protects us against the effects of negative stress by triggering the brain's release of endorphins, the body's natural painkiller.

Spend time with people who enjoy a good laugh. And speaking of laughter, here are some tips to remind you to have fun, hang around people who make you laugh, and take a fun break.

It's important to find something that will excite, motivate and satisfy you. Giving time and talent to help your community or people in need boosts confidence and self-esteem. It gives you a wonderful feeling of accomplishment and reinforces your belief that you are useful and worthwhile.

Maintain strong friendships/relationships/support. There is solid scientific evidence that friendship can extend life. Friendships play a far more important role in maintaining good health and having a long life than most realize. Social ties are the cheapest medicine we've got. Studies attest to the benefits of friendship. People with strong social networks are shown to:

- Boost their chances of surviving life-threatening illness.

- Have stronger, more resilient immune systems.

- Improve their mental health.

- Live longer than people without social ties.

- People with lots of friends are less likely to suffer from depression, anxiety, and other types of mental illness.

Get More Out of Life by creating new relationships. Feeling good about yourself and having a positive relationship with yourself attracts others. People want to be around fun, happy, positive people.

Thoughts to Energize You:

- How you start your day is how you live your day, and how you live your day is how you live your life.

- Starting your day with exercise will keep you in motion all day long. Ten minutes or 10 push-ups are better than nothing at all.

- The body achieves what the mind believes.

- Giving your time and talents to help your community or people in need boosts confidence and self-esteem.

- When you feel your best, it's easier to do your best.

....

Life is either a grand adventure or it's nothing.

....

~Helen Keller

LIFE is
DYNAMIC

---- 8 ----

You are always in the process of growth. As the years pass, you do lose certain roles and responsibilities. You are finished with certain stages of your life. But as a human being, you are never finished. Nothing could be more destructive to the human spirit than the idea that there are no more dreams, no more challenges, and no more exciting experiences.

Grandma Moses was asked by a reporter why she started painting so late in life. She replied, "At 79 I was too old to work in the fields, but I was too young to sit on the porch."

Many people are anxious and fearful about aging. They fear it because it will mean the loss of status, energy, youth, and attractiveness.

Hal Rubenstein, fashion director for In Style Magazine said, "There are two parts to aging, the best part and the worst part. The best part is the wisdom, and the worst part is the mirror. Those bad moments in front of the mirror, can affect your feelings of well-being. Even though the changes are natural and normal, they are often thought of as ugly."

Chances are, if you like the person you see in the mirror every morning, you'll be happier and feel good about yourself.

The image that many people have of older people is that they are incompetent, inflexible, stuck in the past, poor, sick, and slow. With images like these, it's no wonder so many people have come to dislike and fear growing older, and to expect the worst.

Your attitude about aging is the most crucial factor in your adjustment to it. There is more to being young than simply being pretty or being free of wrinkles, gray hair, and age spots. People who are young have inquisitive minds; they are curious and ready to try something new. They enjoy themselves and have fun.

Joan's story

When I was 65-years-old, I lost everything in a house fire. Overnight, 15 years of work was gone: the books I had written, my speaking and promotional material, files, and clients contact information; my desk, with everything on, under, and in it, was destroyed.

Before the fire, I was a positive, confident, and goal-oriented person. After the fire, my only goal was to be safe. As far as I was concerned, my life as a speaker was over. For the first time in my life, I felt old, and without purpose.

Before the fire, I was too busy to think about the fact that I was 65. Afterwards, all the myths I had scoffed at about being 65, came back. "You're old at 65," "It's time to quit," "You're finished"– now they had new meaning for me.

In the days and nights that followed, as I sat in a rented apartment with rented furniture and no personal possessions, I focused on all the negative aspects of aging. I had a problem accepting that anything good was associated with this time in my life.

As my house was being rebuilt, I started looking for books on aging. I wanted to find out if there was anything positive to look forward to. The baby boomers had not yet turned 50, so there was little written about aging.

One day, I read about a study that discovered, "The fastest growing age group in this country are people in their 80s." Eighties! "Well, hot damn, I'm only 65!" It suddenly seemed unthinkable I should waste another moment lamenting my age. Based on my own experience, I realized that in a longer life, we have second and third choices and opportunities to begin again.

Motivational speaker Les Brown reminds us, "You are never too old to set another goal or to dream a new dream."

As long as we live, we need to have hopes, dreams, and aspirations. With health and energy, anyone can have a passion to do something more in this lifetime.

It's important to free yourself from the outdated notions of aging. You must be unafraid and daring and willing to take risks, and be willing to break the mold of aging that reflects a less-than-positive view of your own aging.

One of the things you can do is to connect with other women. The women around you can provide important insights that will help in your desire to evolve. Getting together with other women, to talk about changes that are happening in yourself, is crucial, particularly since our youth-oriented culture doesn't yet support or appreciate people who are getting older.

The aging myths you hold about physical and mental vitality are not only destructive in themselves, they add to the belief that the third stage of life doesn't allow for further growth. Sharing your feelings with other women who are experiencing the same changes will help you understand and accept those changes in yourself. You need to keep an open mind and never stop doing or trying new things.

The two important qualities in successful agingare self-confidence and a good self-image. Unfortunately, these are two things you may begin to lose as you age. With the loss of these two qualities, you're not as sure of yourself as you once were, and you don't feel as good about yourself as you once did.

Everything changes based on how we perceive it. If you want to believe aging is terrible and that you are doomed to live your life in misery and depression, then you will not be disappointed.

- Dr. Gayle Olinekava

When you are confident, it frees you of unnecessary worry and fear. It helps you to make decisions, formulate creative ideas, cultivate new relationships, and take the necessary risks in life. Self-confidence is the ingredient that results in self-assurance and the conviction that you can deal successfully with life and its challenges. When you are confident, you have a deep innerbelief in your abilities and in your importance as a human being. Projecting confidence is a matter of being in control of the messages you send.

People don't know how you feel unless you send them messages that tell them you're not sure of yourself. Eye contact and the way you walk, talk, and act, often communicate these messages.

One of the greatest things you need to be aware of is that as long as you live, you have the privilege of growth. You can learn new skills, engage in new kinds of work, meet new people, and have new relationships. It also comes from knowing who you are and what is possible. It's important to keep in mind that there is always room for creative thought, new options and new discoveries. The benefits derived from being self-confident tend to support what you already have. In general, the stronger your feelings, the more satisfied you are with your life. This gives you the power to embrace life. If you use youth as the only measurement of how good you feel, you will experience feelings of worthlessness and doubt as you show signs of growing older.

Everybody's growing older. Confidence really isn't a matter of age or appearance, it is an attitude. For some people, confidence only gets stronger as they age. And you are not only living longer, you are entering old age later in life. Taking a positive view of your own aging is the only sane decision you can make.

Life is much too short to live with the fear of growing older. For a long life, it's important to continue to develop all aspects of yourself – mentally, physically, and spiritually.

You are as young as your faith, as old as your doubts, as young as your confidence, as old as your fears, as young as your hope, as old as your despair.

– Samual Ultman

Ask yourself, "What are the simple, easy activities I can do each day that will have a great impact on my health, my personal development, and my life?"

Examples:

- Exercise.

- Meditate.

- Journal.

- Read five to ten pages of self-improvement books each day.

• Say your affirmations daily.

This list will also help you stay strong, vibrant, and resilient for years to come. You need to take the time to decide what you want your life to be – what you want it to look like in the next year, or five years from now. Ask yourself, "What can I change inside myself and in my world ... now?"

To reposition yourself, or to find a new direction, it's helpful for you to spend time alone, in quiet contemplation. Find some unfamiliar environment to help break the connection with the routine aspects of your life, to gain a new perspective.

You need to ask yourself, "What is unique about me?" Write down three positive statements that describe you:

• One thing I am able to do well.

- One special characteristic I possess.

- One special talent I have.

To change things in your life is a matter of changing your beliefs about them. It is the key to unlocking the hidden potential dormant within you. You also need to keep reminding yourself, it isn't who I am, it's who I think I am, that sets the boundaries of my accomplishments."

Everyone is here to live life successfully in one way or another. You have been given a purpose for your life, but that's not all. You've also been given the talents to fulfill that purpose. You have been given your identity, your own uniqueness. Never before has anyone appeared on the face of the earth with a combination of your qualities, abilities, and talents.

Julie's story

In the past year, my grandmother gave me all of the sympathy cards we received after my mother's death (when I was nine years old). One of them in particular has been of huge importance to me and will be for the rest of my life. The sympathy card was from my mother's place of employment, Central State Prison. The inmates and staff sent a card and poem depicting the way they felt about my mother, Dianne.

The poem read ...
We'll miss your smile at the beginning of every day, we'll miss the way you treated us like human-beings regardless of the mistakes we've made in life. We'll miss you the way you treated us as though we mattered not as though we were just matter. We'll miss you Dianne, your lightheartedness and easy going attitude. We'll miss you Dianne.

We appreciated you perhaps even more than anyone else; we couldn't afford taking you for granted. Therefore your kindness always meant a lot to us. You were beautiful people, everyday people, unchanging from day to day. Everyday we'll miss you, no longer will that bright spot in our day be there. We'll miss you Dianne, but never forget you.

Why this poem means so much to me: be who you are, treat others with love and kindness no matter their circumstances.

Now is the time to ask yourself: What haven't I done yet in my life? What opportunities are waiting for me?

Remember, you have the freedom to reinvent yourself and to release the powers of your creative mind, and in doing so, discover a new sense of purpose.

Ahead of you may stretch 20, 30, or [even] more, productive years of possibilities and opportunities. There are no age restrictions on getting more out of life.

Thoughts to Energize You:

- Chances are, if you like the person you see in the mirror every morning, you'll be happier and feel good about yourself.

- Projecting confidence is a matter of being in control of the messages you send.

- Everybody's growing older, but you don't have to be old.

- Accepting the changes that come with aging creates a solid foundation for self–esteem, confidence, and self-worth.

- Ahead of you may stretch 20, 30, or [even] more, productive years of possibilities and opportunities.

- There are no age restrictions on getting more out of life.

....

I've learned that people forget what you said,
people will forget what you did, but people will
never forget the way you made them feel.

....

~Maya Angelou

How is Joan, at the age of 92, currently getting more out of life?

- I'm in the process of writing two more books.

- I have speaking engagements in my future.

- My two daughters and I are setting up a new business. The name of our company is "The Trashy Women." We will sell antiques, collectables, furniture, and interesting old stuff. To begin with, we will have two sales a year. It will be fun.

- I have the privilege of having a lot of friends … of all ages. We get together as often as we can.

- I spend time with my family. I have a son and three daughters, one daughter-in-law, and three sons-in-law. I have 11 grandchildren and 20 great-grandchildren. With them, I can truly say I'm getting more out of life.

How is Julie, at the age of 39, currently getting more out of life?

- Drinking my morning cup of coffee every day (no coffee, no workee).

- Exercising.

- Being a parent to a 2- and 5-year-old – wait, or are they taking the life out of me? Just kidding, love them dearly.

- Having mentors and/or friends of all ages.

- Cuddling with Earl and Clark (my two Great Danes).

- Having a supportive and loving husband.

- Meeting new, inspiring people.

- Listening to self-improvement books on CDs on my way to and from work.

- Surrounding myself with loving, kind people who fill me up with joy and compassion.

Acknowledgments

We would like to extend our deepest thanks and appreciation to a number of people who made a special contribution with their ideas and insights.

To Patty Kennedy Bronstien for your editing and personal involvement in this project.

To Marnie Kennedy for all your help with chapter arrangements and ideas for this book

My special thanks to Gloria VanDemmeltraadt for your suggestions and the final editing of this book.

To Melissa McGath at Voom Creative for her and her team's amazing design work. Our success is directly related to the time, talent, and energy she consistently provides in all she does for us.

To my husband Brent and children Dianna and Aaron.

About the Authors

Joan Kennedy is a strong and insightful speaker. Her content is rich with personal experiences, optimism, and humor. She continues to draw rave reviews from audiences of all ages, delivering a powerful message that life is for living now and the goal for all of us is a life of good health, productivity, fun, and laughter.

Living life and defying the myths of aging, Joan Kennedy has spent a lifetime battling life's adversities with humor, grit, and joy. Joan has published four books. The third and fourth books are "What's Age Got to Do With It?" and "Unlocking the Secrets of Successful Women." She also produced several booklets and a CD for babies called "Lull-a-Baby," which is a collection of lullabies filled with positive and loving messages.

Joan has spread her philosophy with books and speaking engagements across the country. She has worked with major corporations, health care organizations, conventions, and conferences and groups of all sizes and ages.

Three major factors in living the good life with energy and productivity are simply:

- Protect your health at all costs.

- Have a positive attitude.

- Keep your dreams alive, and set goals for your future.

Joan has spent more than 35 years striding across stages with energy and enthusiasm, proudly billing herself as the "oldest female motivational speaker in the country."

Julie Lother is living her passion, inspiring people every day to live a better life. She holds a Bachelor's Degree in Exercise Science and has more than 15 years of experience in fitness and wellness industries. She is a certified yoga instructor, inspiring personal trainer, and business entrepreneur. Julie's business name, "Fit 2b Well," speaks to who she is and how she lives. She uniquely blends her knowledge and exercise to create programs, classes, and workshops that bring mind and body together for positive change, inspiring people to live their most authentic lives. She incorporates new ways of thinking into classes and programs on positive living, teaching people to manifest and create the lives they desire.

She believes all people can change ... they just need to set their minds to it. Through her coaching, she has witnessed, first hand, personal growth and transformation at all levels. She is driven by her ability to love and care for the well-being of others and push them toward personal success.

Made in the USA
San Bernardino, CA
29 February 2016